THE DOGFATHER

MY LOVE OF DOGS, DESSERTS AND GROWING UP ITALIAN

ISBN# : 978-0-578-74752-1

Dedication

To all the women of my life:

My caring wife Bessy who opened my heart and our
home to rescue dogs.

My mother and grandmother who provided tables
full of desserts for me to make memories around.

My amazing sisters who keep that
tradition alive with the next generation.

My beautiful daughter Milana who knows nothing
but love for dogs....and desserts.

With a very special thanks to Michael Pullano, Julianna Carfaro
and Erica Beltran whose assistance made this book possible.

Introduction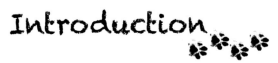

As long as I could remember, I've had a deep love for desserts. I wasn't even a fat kid. Everyone would always say my metabolism was off the charts because of the amount I ate, I should have been a complete chub. Italian pastries always had a place in my home. Whenever there was going to be company at our house, or we were going for a visit to a family member's house, my father and I would go and get pastries. That was my toy store growing up. I would be so excited to take a trip with him. Pushing the door open and hearing the little bell ring, was my version of the round one bell of a heavyweight fight. I'd charge in and start swinging. There was nothing like pressing my nose up to the glass and hand picking what pastries would make the cut to be part of the dozen we ordered. I'd be specific, annoyingly so. Like asking to see the third cannoli from the back, and then deciding whether or not it was good enough to be added to the collection I was curating.

After the choices were made, I'd be proud of the sweetness I assembled. Watching them wrap the red and white string around that plain white box to seal it was always a satisfying part of the dessert outing. It was like a lock placed on a vault of happiness that once we opened a delightful experience would start. I would proudly present the pastry to those we were about to indulge with, as if I baked them myself. I took full responsibility. Which was odd, because I did not bake them and did not pay for them, so it was an odd sense of entitlement.

Fast forward forty years and it is still my favorite way to spend time with people. Break out the coffee and desserts and I'm home baby. It's become such a part of my personality that it is what a lot of people know me for. When going out to eat with family or friends, the desserts are always a course. And they are never optional. The answer 100% of the time when a waiter or waitress comes over and asks "Would you like to see a dessert menu?" is a resounding yes.

Without fail whoever I am seated with at the table will look to me knowing we are about to get into it. At restaurants, I like hosting my own personal Venetian hour with multiple desserts complete with side plates and extra forks to be able to split them up amongst the group.

My stance is that deep down everyone always wants to ask for dessert but no one wants to ask for it. That's where I come in. I am the mouthpiece for those desiring something sweet at the end of the meal. Dessert is the most exciting of the courses that turns regular dinners into feasts. An exclamation point of the meal if you will, providing the final taste in your mouth when you get up from the table. It leaves a mark of deliciousness on the evening.

I must admit I am raising my children in the same fashion. One of my son's first words was dessert. That is not a joke. I was super proud. I think because I always enjoyed eating with my dad, that for sure put me on a path of raising my children in a similar fashion. A common phrase before bedtime in my home is "But wait, we didn't have dessert" as if it is impossible for the day to be done without it.

My love of desserts is rivaled only by my love of dogs, specifically rescues. Rescue is my favorite breed. Once I got my first rescue pup, it was off to the races. At the time I am writing this, I currently have

dogs (with an additional two that have passed on) and I never thought in a million years I would have a full blown pack living in my home. Nor did I think I was the guy that would be buying them matching pajamas for Christmas morning. But here we are friends. I am the alpha male to a pack of dogs I love dearly and are attached to me at the hip. Literally…they all sleep on me. When it comes time for me to go on the road for work, they sense it and I can't even pack my suitcase without them being all over my clothes.

All the Gatto Pups are featured in this book. I struck a deal with my wife from our first dog. We can get them if I can name them. So my running theme became naming them after desserts. It's fun and they make great names. Not all dessert names do mind you. I don't have a dog named Flan or Bread Pudding. No offense to those desserts. I just don't think I'd want to be running around my neighborhood yelling "Bread Pudding!" if he got out of the yard. Not that yelling Biscotti is much better, but to each their own. So in this book, I'll be highlighting some of my favorite desserts, sharing a memory or two, and tell you a little about my correlating dog to said dessert.

I also wanted to do everything for this project on my own. I always loved photography, so I took all the pictures and designed all the sets. I wrote the book on my own and even taught myself a book design program and self-published it. Seemed like the perfect time to start a project, since the world basically had stopped with the Covid-19 crisis of 2020. I mean pictures of dogs and desserts are a delicious combination after all. Enjoy and Bone Appétit! See what I did there — expect lots more dog puns coming your way.

Cannoli

The cannoli is ingrained in every aspect of my life. My favorite dessert. The name of my production company. My first family dog as an adult. If I didn't choose it for the name of my first dog there's a good chance my first born child would've been Cannoli Gatto. One of my favorite cannoli stories is when my first nephew, Anthony, was about three years old, he'd love to eat desserts with me. It was our thing. After a meal, we got silly at dessert time and were putting cream on each other's faces. He was double fisting cannolis and going bite for bite on the delicious cream on top of each one.

As he feasted, the cream from the one he was holding in his right hand fell from the top and landed in front of him on the table. He looked at his two hands and saw they were full, and knew if he put one down on the table to retrieve it, I'd most certainly eat the unguarded cannoli. So Anthony decided to simply drop his head down and vacuum clean the dollop of cream with his mouth right off the table. I roared with laughter as I bursted with pride that, as an uncle, I taught my nephew the importance of desserts and protecting what is rightfully yours.

When my wife Bessy and I started getting serious while dating, we decided to take it to the next level and get a dog. There was this little puppy shop in Lynbrook, New York which we frequented when coming out to Long Island to visit my sister. It would help Bessy get her puppy fix instead of accosting a random stranger's dog on the streets of the city. At the shop they would let you hold them and play with them. The bin in the front of the shop was a cuteness overload of fluffy puppies tumbling and playing over one another. Inside were Teddy Bear breed puppies, which are a mix of a Shih Tzu and Bichon Frise. Bessy had her heart set on one little fellow and kept petting him. Whenever I went to pet him, this cute little brown and white puppy would come over and lean on my arm (not that you'd know Cannoli had any brown in her as a puppy since she is a snowball now). She nuzzled right up to me every time I put my hand in. At one point she actually closed her eyes and took a little snooze resting on the back of my hand as the boy pup that Bessy loved chewed and jumped all over the place. I asked a worker there to let us hold this little napper, and Bessy even said to me that was the wrong one when the employee pulled her from the pen. But I just asked Bessy to go sit and hold her. Within minutes this little white angel cotton ball canine was asleep on Bessy and I knew that was going to be our first dog.

We had recently moved into our own place together, so I asked Bessy if she wanted to take it home and she responded "Are you sure?" Side note, years later she would ask me the same thing when I proposed to her on the beach in the Caribbean. I assured her that I was, however there was a catch. The deal was that she can have it as long as I can name it. We shook on it and the first Gatto Pup came into existence. After much deliberation, I landed between two of my favorite foods. Ravioli and Cannoli. The dog shared two properties of the cannoli, being white and instantly bringing a smile to my face. So the name was decided and Cannoli was added to our family as our first furry child. On occasion, Bessy would even dress her up in little doggy clothing which I was never on board with totally.

With her being our first dog, we had a strict rule that the dog did not sleep in the bed. Cannoli had a little bed in the corner of my closet. But whenever I was at work or away on business, the dog would nap and sleep with Bessy in the bed. So that rule went the way of the dodo. It didn't seem like a problem then, but fast forward to now when I have a half dozen dogs, that's no longer the case. The nighttime real estate in my bed is quite the challenge. I share my side and even my pillow with them. It's a disaster.

As far as personality goes, Cannoli is my most skittish dog. She's afraid of loud noises, cardboard boxes, thunder and fireworks. We found that out the hard way on Memorial Day of that year. My niece and nephew were in their middle school marching band and we decided to watch the Lynbrook Town Parade on Main Street. Cannoli was with us looking adorable with a red, white and blue bow in her hair. As soon as the marching band started to play and the booming drums came close, Cannoli started climbing up Bessy and out of fear started pooping. Bessy was covered and just started screaming and ran four blocks to my sister's house to clean herself and our little puppy up.

Cannoli is also arguably my most beautiful. She actually had a doggie modeling agent for a while and landed a few gigs. She was booked in a Target advertisement and a holiday catalog for a baby clothing company. So she's a bit of a diva. And I know what you're thinking. "Joe you shopped, you didn't adopt!"

In all honesty, much like most of the public I was completely uneducated and had no idea about the world of puppy mills and the thousands upon thousands of dogs needing homes in shelters. But I quickly learned first hand the complications that come with these types of dogs. Within the first year, Cannoli had cost me thousands of dollars in vet visits and testing and surgeries. It really opened my eyes to the world of animal rescue and I never turned back. And also kind of my motivation to put her to work to contribute to the household income.

Biscotti

When it comes to drinking coffee, I'm a dunker. I rarely have a cup of coffee without a treat to dunk in it. I love a good biscotti. A fun one. Almonds, chocolate dipped, pistachio. Whatevs. My grandmother's sister used to bake them when I was growing up. We called her Aunt Irene Taralli. A taralli is a type of cookie-cracker that went great with milk. When I was younger and we'd go to visit, she'd sit me down with a big plate of them and a tall glass of milk. That's where my love of dunking cookies was born. Oh, and of course the Oreo. Can't forget the Oreo.

Biscotti is my first rescue dog. And it was quite a serendipitous chain of events that occurred to make it all happen. I was at work filming my television show "Impractical Jokers" in a park by the Brooklyn Bridge in lower Manhattan. We were playing shoe shine guys with a stand set up on the lawn. It's a location we had shot our hidden camera show a thousand times before. As we were getting ready to film, a text message came in from my wife with the link to an adorable 1-year-old puppy at Animal Haven, a shelter located not too far from where we were filming.

I fell in love with her sad little face right away. Bessy really fell in love and wanted us to go see her that day. The problem was the shelter closed at 5 pm and I wasn't done filming until 6 pm. The police have only been called on us twice while making our show. A park-goer we were interacting with didn't appreciate our jokes, so he complained to the park police. When the cops checked our permit, they found discrepancies which made us close up shop. To this date, nine seasons in, this is the ONLY time this ever happened. It was 3 pm. I called Bessy, told her to grab our dog Cannoli and meet me at Animal Haven to go see the dog.

When we got there, Biscotti was terrified. Her tail was between her legs and we were not allowed to go near her because she was aggressive when frightened. So we just sat on the floor in the meeting room as she sat on the other side glued to the volunteer helping us. Eventually she walked over to Cannoli, started sniffing and immediately her tail went up. She began hopping around to play. I was hesitant due to her trust issues, but knew with some love and a good home she'd be ok. As soon as we got to the house, Cannoli and Biscotti jumped on the couch and sat side by side for hours. Later, as I was sitting on the couch watching TV, she jumped on my lap, curled up and fell asleep. We've been inseparable ever since.

Biscotti is hands down my sweetest dog. Everyone falls in love with her. Her sweeping tail and fat little body are a killer cuteness combination. Plus she is all about the naps and snuggles, and not only with humans but the other dogs too. For goodness sake, she even plays
peek-a-boo!

We always joke in my house that in our next life we want to come back as Biscotti. What makes her my favorite (don't worry, the other dogs know), is that she proved to me what rescue could do. She unconditionally loves me and is always excited to be with me. That scared little broken dog is a thing of the past, and this loving thriving silly puppy is one of the favorite things to come home to. She's also the momma bear, the alpha of our pack. Where she goes, the other dogs go. If she gives a little growl, the other dogs stop dead in their tracks. She has gone from that scared pup in the corner to the leader of a happy pack and that has been the most magical thing to witness.

Then There Were Two

The relationship between Cannoli and Biscotti is so interesting to me. They bonded instantly. I think because Cannoli was taken from her mom so young due to the puppy mill practices and Biscotti was lonely and afraid, they found a real love for each other. For the first couple years, they would not leave each other's side. And when together, they straight up cuddled.

They found comfort in having each other, and their bond set the tone as the pack expanded. Biscotti took on the role of the "momma bear", where Cannoli always taught the newest member of the furry family to trust Biscotti and follow what she did. It warms my heart that our home brought them together.

Mishkeen

This dog was my delicious mess. And the most delicious mess of a dessert I know is an old family recipe. We call it "Ice Box Cake." My grandmother would make it for my mother and her siblings on their birthdays when they were children. It's a layered cake, made of whipped cream, chocolate pudding, strawberry jello and a graham cracker crust. Nothing special, but they grew up pretty poor and it was a special occasion cake. And it is hands down one of my favorite desserts because it reminds me of family and tradition. I also love the taste. It's a simple pleasure. I don't think there has been an occasion, where it was a big family get together or holiday, where an Ice Box Cake was not on the menu.

Now back to the dog. As far as the name goes, Mishkeen is not a dessert. It is a saying my grandparents used to say when they saw something pitiful or something that needed help, as in "awww… that poor thing." So it was a no brainer to name this little guy Mishkeen.

I never thought in a million years I'd ever adopt a senior dog. And what an adorable mess this angry little elf of a dog was. Full disclosure, I never would have adopted him if it wasn't for Bessy. She totally pushed him onto the family. My only hope was that Biscotti would reject him and I'd have that excuse that he wasn't welcome to the pack. But Biscotti's sweet loving side won the day and we took Mishkeen home. He was partially deaf, blind and had no teeth. He was 4 pounds, three pounds of it being his tongue. It always hung out of his mouth. He had slight dementia and he loved to attack. But with no teeth, it was a pretty fruitless exercise. He'd basically gum you and growl. It was very entertaining. He also introduced me to the world of senior doggy diapers, which I did not know was even a thing.

We only had Mishkeen for seven months, but he arguably provided more entertainment and family stories than every other dog combined. A stand out moment for sure was the pool incident. We had an inground pool and one day he decided to walk right off the edge and fall into it. I laughed at first, thinking he could doggy paddle his way to safety. But he sunk like an anchor and I had to dive into the pool fully clothed to save him. The next day, I went on Amazon and got him a doggy life jacket. In a million years I never thought this product was something that would end up being added to my cart.

He was not pretty, friendly or nice. But you couldn't help but to smile when looking at his ridiculous face with that silly tongue. He definitely made an impact on our home and hearts in the short time he was a Gatto Pup.

The
Epic
Tongue

Ice Box Cake Recipe

Ingredients:

* 1 box of Strawberry Jello mix

* 1 box of Cook to Serve chocolate pudding mix

* 1 tub of "Cool Whip"

* Graham Crackers

* Lasagna tin pan

Instructions:

1. Line the bottom of the tin with a layer of Graham Crackers

2. Follow the instructions to prepare chocolate pudding mix

3. Pour the chocolate pudding into the tin on top of the graham cracker layer then place the tin in the refrigerator for 20 minutes

4. While the pudding is cooling, prepare the strawberry jello mix

5. Slowly pour the jello mix over the pudding, using the back of a spoon to stop the stream of Jello from breaking pudding

6. Place the tin back into the refrigerator for another two hours to let fully cool

7. Before serving, layer the top with Cool Whip and enjoy!

Tartufo

The tartufo is in an exclusive grouping of one of the very few ice cream desserts I enjoy. I do not really like ice cream. I know, by the looks of me, you would never think that was the truth. However, the chocolate covered ice cream ball known as a tartufo is right up my alley. Otherwise it's not my thing. Like whenever I go to one of those "make your own" sundae type places, my cup always ends up with the smallest dollop of ice cream and the rest of the cup filled with twenty toppings, ranging from rainbow sprinkles to Reeses Pieces to hot fudge. Maybe subconsciously I am terrified of ice cream headaches.

The first time I ordered a tartufo, I was in my early twenties on a date at a restaurant in Little Italy. As I normally do, I ordered a couple of desserts to split. Having no idea what a tartufo actually was, they put it on the table. My date was lactose intolerant. So I enjoyed the dessert on my own, and honestly that was the best part of the evening.

Tartufo the dog became a Gatto Pup basically without me knowing. I was on the road for work and missed a Mother's Day. So Bessy decided to cheer herself up by going to a puppy charity event and low and behold, found herself another furry baby. A few days later we went to the shelter to see her, unbeknownst to me that Bessy had already filled out the paperwork and we were actually picking her up to come home with us. Mind you we had just gotten Mishkeen two weeks before, so we went from two to four dogs in two weeks. Enter Tartufo. I've never felt anything like her coat. It is like petting a cloud, honestly. She is the softest thing on earth. And she straight up hugs you. Arms over your shoulder as if you are slow dancing. The night of the charity event where Bessy met her, that's what she did. And now she became the third sister.

She's my biggest dog and certainly my most awkward. She has no idea how to lay on someone to snuggle, always comes in butt first. Plus, she has these really long legs so it always ends up being such an odd position. But she is all love. Such a loving and attentive dog and super appreciative of being rescued. She must be pet and/or on top of someone at all times. There is no subtle way for her to do it either. Her tactics include army crawling her way toward you if you are in bed, or if you are petting another dog she does this thing where she will insert her head where you are currently petting and basically steal the pets.

Zeppole

Growing up in New York City, there was nothing like the San Gennaro Feast in Little Italy. It was an event that provided some of my most cherished childhood memories. My family would drive into Manhattan from Staten Island and against all odds, my father would always find a parking spot extremely close to our destination right on the street. It was a gift, one I inherited and that always impresses my friends by the way. But I digress. As we walked down Mulberry street and passed all the food vendors, I could not wait to get a bag of zeppoles with powdered sugar. It was heaven in a bag. So that made the sweet taste of those fried sugary dough balls even more sweet. I'd dive in and come out looking like Pablo Escobar. A treat well worth the mess. And for a long time in my life, I would only get them this time of the year.

When the time came for another senior (after Mishkeen had crossed the rainbow bridge) we met the most awesome little bear cub of a dog. He had recently undergone surgery to remove an eye because of owner neglect. As a result of being a breeding dog at a puppy mill, spending his life in a cramped cage, the lower part of his front legs barely worked. Despite these things he was such a love bug. Whenever you started to give him scratches he'd grunt and collapse right there, soaking up the human interaction. His fur was thick and silky and so enjoyable to pet that it was a win win for all parties involved.

He wasn't a big dog for a King Charles Cavalier mix, but he was extremely dense. The dog loved nothing more than napping. And he'd be happiest when it was time to take him upstairs for bed. He couldn't go up stairs, so I would carry him up every night and I swear I'd see him smile at me as we ascended the stairs and I placed him on the bed. Zeppole also broke the mold for Gatto Pups. He was my first non-white dog. I certainly had a type when it came to the dogs I rescued. Small, white and fluffy. But there was no denying that Zeppole was meant to be mine. He lived out his days comfortably and provided much love to our family, especially my daughter Milana who was two at the time. She would love to cuddle him and we'd often find her on the floor curled up next to him. I credit their relationship as the start of her love for dogs.

Best Buds

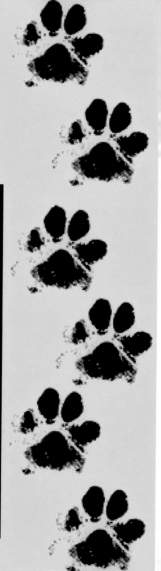

Spumoni

Spumoni is a kind of specialty ice cream that's a mix of three different flavors: Pistachio, Chocolate and Vanilla. When I was younger, you couldn't get it everywhere. There was a place in Staten Island called "Ralph's Italian Ices" in my neighborhood that had it. It was a stand alone ice cream parlor that served street side, meaning you did not go inside the store. There were front windows and you ordered directly from the cashier when you walked up. Kind of like a drive thru ice cream parlor that you walked up to instead of driving through. After you got your frozen treat, patrons would sit on the hoods of their cars in the parking lot and eat their ice cream as it was quickly melting out of those white paper cups. Spumoni was my mother's favorite flavor, so growing up it was always a treat when she would share hers with me. Many a summer night my family would lie on the hood of my father's car looking up at the stars and just talk and laugh as we devoured the frozen yumminess.

Sometimes the universe connects the dots in the most random ways that you are forced to believe it was meant to be. That's the story of me and my pup Spumoni.

A couple years back, I was on the road touring the west coast for the weekend. We were playing Las Vegas, then Arizona, and ending in Los Angeles. As part of the night in Vegas, I was doing some press interviews. One of the outlets was with the organization #LOVEPUP, who's tactic is an extremely smart and simple one. They ask people in the public eye with large social media followings to come take photos with dogs looking for homes and post them to spread awareness. I was being interviewed while holding a different dog and Spumoni came over curled up and fell asleep in my lap.

Her story was that she was a bait dog recovered in a neighborhood in Arizona notorious for pit bull fighting rings. Bait dogs are small puppies that dog fighters use to train their dogs to kill. It's a disgusting, heartbreaking reality. Spumoni was found sleeping under a dumpster with two male puppies. I fell in love instantly and told the man that ran the organization "I'm taking this one home." He told me "that's not how it works" to which my friend Brian replied, "That's how it works if you're Joe Gatto." However, time was not on my side. I had to be on stage in two hours and I was leaving town on a 9:00 am flight the next day. I told them I'd pick the dog up the next morning at 7:30 AM on my way to the airport.

When I got back to the hotel I called the local PetSmart and asked if they delivered. The woman who answered the phone laughed out loud, rightfully so, and told me they didn't. I then asked her if she watched a television show called Impractical Jokers, to which she replied "I love that show." I explained to her that I was Joe and trying to adopt a dog before I leave tomorrow. She was hesitant to believe me but after she checked the internet to see that we were indeed in town that night playing the MGM and after I yelled "Larry" a couple times for her to verify my identity, she agreed to put it all together and deliver to my hotel concierge. A true hero. The next morning I was all set to grab the puppy and boom, Spumoni was mine.

My family was meeting me in Los Angeles to spend a couple of days vacationing. So I came into the hotel room to meet my wife, daughter and 5 month old son with this brand new puppy. My daughter flipped out and started playing with her. She shrieked with joy as Spumoni jumped on her and licked in excitement. My wife's reaction was not as warm. She looked at me as she held my crying son with a look that was a combination of surprise, disbelief, and just a touch of rage. But once I traded her the puppy for my son, she came around very quickly to Team Spumoni. And the rest is history.

Spumoni, a Yorkie Terrier mix, is my most loyal dog. She loves me with every hair on her body. And she is my travel buddy because she's compact, so it's easy. I often take her along when traveling for work when doing speaking engagements or tours to provide a little comfort of home on the road. Every night when it's bedtime she makes a little nest between my knees and curls up in the most adorable little way. Just like the first time we met.

Then There Were Five

With the addition of Spumoni to the pack, the Gatto Pups now outnumbered the Gatto humans. The WiFi network name in my home was changed to "The Doghouse" to commemorate the event. And I needed back up during feeding time so it became a family affair.

Pignoli

Italian cookie trays were a staple at our house. But during the holidays, one specific cookie would come hot on the scene, crispy and clean. Enter the pignoli, the king of the cookie tray at its epicenter. The pastry shop we used to get these trays from growing up would put a limited amount of those delicious treasures in the batch, so you had to act fast once the tray was placed on the table. They were also my Pop-Pop's favorite, so whenever we opened the cellophane and exposed the pile of cookies, he'd get first dibs and take two of them. I used to play a game where my grandmother would make me walk his dessert plate over to him while he was sipping his coffee and I'd sneak one of the nuts right off the top of the cookie right in front of him and eat it. And he'd tickle me trying to get it back.

The latest senior dog in the Gatto Pup pack is Pignoli. When the rotating number 5 spot (our senior spot) opened up after Zeppole left us, this fragile little monster came into the mix. Full disclosure, she's not cute. From the right angle, she is straight up scary to be honest. Like horror movie, what the hell is that lurking in the shadows, run for your life it's a Zombie dog frightening. Just standing there in the doorway with her one

eye and then slow-walking toward you like a Maltese version of the girl from "The Ring." But she makes your heart bleed for her. A definite survivor. The shelter we got her from told us they had found her in a tenement building in the Bronx living in the stairwell on the Fourth of July. So I'm happy to give her a home with a big fluffy bed and lots of food and treats to ride out her days. But I do wish she'd stop barking at 3:30AM every morning and scaring the hell out of me when I am half asleep and see her coming through a doorway. She also kind of walks sideways, or crabesque if you will. Her equilibrium is off so she hardly walks a straight line. It's safe to say if she ever got pulled over by the police she would not pass a sobriety test. One of the many reasons I don't let her drive.

She wears a diaper, which I find hysterical. And we have to have baby gates up in my house to protect her from falling down steps since she can't see them and just keeps walking forward. In full transparency we found that out the hard way when she Wile E. Coyote'd off my dining room stairs and fell down a few. But she is resilient the little grandma. And when she curls up into a little ball on her big poof of a bed it does make you feel warm and fuzzy. Although I must admit I constantly check to see if she's still breathing.

Napoleon

The only other pastry in the white box that would rival a cannoli for me is the Napoleon. First off, they are a work of art and so inviting. And the ratio of flaky goodness to cream is perfection. Here's a fat guy trick I'd like to share with my readers that blew my mind. If you are going to cut a Napoleon to share, turn it on its side. That move will prevent it from just squishing down and all the cream overflowing from the side. You're welcome.

The Napoleon killed my game with the ladies hard in my teen years. Let me explain. I was not a good looking teen, gawky AF with braces for four years. It wasn't so much that my teeth were that messed up, but more so that I was the last of three children to go to my family orthodontist. So I think he wanted to milk my father's insurance as far as it could go knowing that the Gatto jacked up teeth money train was pulling into the station. Eating a Napoleon is messy for sure. But it is a disaster for a metal mouth. In eighth grade, I went to a birthday party and a crush of mine, Christine, was there. We were a classmate of mine and I was quite smitten with her.

When the desserts were put out, I shared a Napoleon with her and it was the highlight of my pre-teen years. The problem was that the Napoleon was so messy and sticky that my braces were overthrown by this French Revolution in my mouth. I got so self conscious that I pretended to be sick and have my mom come get me early. Damn you Napoleon and your tempting deliciousness.

As far as the dog goes, Napoleon ranks right up there with Spumoni as an impulse adoption. But this time, Bessy was with me so I don't take all the blame. I was receiving an award at the annual New York Animal Care Center's Gala and he was there walking around meeting guests. I took to him right away and he followed me around the ballroom filled with one thousand guests. As if to say, "You're not getting rid of me." When people tried to pet him, he'd keep walking over to me. There was no escaping the fact that this good boy was to be mine. During my acceptance speech I announced that I was taking him home and I swear I could see his signature ears perk up with delight. When we came home that night from the gala to introduce him to the pack, it was a bit hectic. So I slept in the guest room with just him and I, and he cuddled right in and slept like a baby. I've had him for about six months now and he's totally been welcomed as one of the pack.

A big change the addition of Napoleon to the Gatto Pups did was expand the upper limit of our pack to six. There had never been more than five canines. But he adds something for sure. And as my wife says if you have two, you can have ten. Napoleon is definitely my most "dog" dog. He runs, plays, chews, digs, barks and is always on the move. It must be because he's got German Shepherd in him. It's funny to watch the other dogs look up from their naps on the couch to be like "chill out." He's also my puppy and tests my patience a bit. But he is super smart and learning the ways of the house. He'll be fat and lazy before you know it.

Day Ones

One of the most exciting parts of rescue is the first day you have with your newest furry family members. The hapiness you feel on the "freedom ride" home from the shelter is born out of gratitude and excitement. I've had such a great experience over the years being able to give a home to so many special loving animals. I encourage you all to do the same. There truly is no feeling in the world like the love of a rescue.

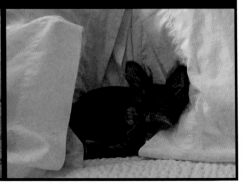

Adopt Dont Shop

Here are some of the great organizations that I've come to know and love working with to help animals in need. Feel free to check them out and support them if you can. They are champions for what they do.

The world's largest no-kill animal rescue and adoption organization. Located in Port Washington, New York. I got Zeppole through them.

http://www.animalleague.org

#LOVEPUP

Founded by 104.7 KISS FM's Johnjay Van Es and his family, the #LovePup Foundation is a non-profit dog rescue organization in Arizona. I got Spumoni through them.

http://www.lovepupfoundation.org

We strive to find loving homes for homeless and abandoned cats, dogs, and rabbits. Our mission is to end animal homelessness in NYC! I got Tartufo and Napoleon through them.

https://www.nycacc.org

We find homes for abandoned cats and dogs in New York City and throughout the Tri-State area, and provide behavior intervention when needed to improve chances of adoption. I got Biscotti, Mishkeen and Pignoli through them.

https://www.animalhaven.org

Best Friends Animal Society, founded in its present form in 1993, is an American nonprofit 501 animal welfare organization. The group does outreach nationwide with shelters, rescue groups and members to promote pet adoption, no-kill animal rescue, and spay-and-neuter practices. They get an honorable mention from me as I have not adopted through them....yet.

http://www.bestfriends.org